Mr Bevan's Dream

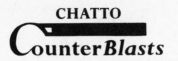

CHATTO
CounterBlasts

Sue

TOWNSEND

Mr Bevan's
Dream

Chatto & Windus
LONDON

Published in 1989 by
Chatto & Windus Ltd
30 Bedford Square
London WC1B 3SG

A CIP catalogue record for this book
is available from the British Library

ISBN 0 7011 3468 2

Photoset in Linotron Ehrhardt by
Rowland Phototypesetting Ltd
Bury St Edmunds, Suffolk
Printed in Great Britain by
St Edmundsbury Press Ltd
Bury St Edmunds, Suffolk

Introduction

LIKE MOST of my friends I was an Easter leaver, which meant in my case that I left my secondary modern school one week before my fifteenth birthday. I have no formal educational qualifications. I can't remember anyone mentioning G C Es. When I was twenty-three I attended a part-time course in youth and community work. The course lasted three years and *attended* was the relevant word. The certificates I was given at the end of the course – in child psychology, adolescent psychology and youth and community work – pronounce only that I attended the course. There is no mention of passing or attaining a nationally recognised qualification. I enjoyed the course, it got me out of the house once a week and gave me something to think about other than the nappy bucket.

My tutor in psychology was a brown-robed Franciscan brother. I thought his lectures were brilliant but most of my fellow students thought he was barmy (perhaps he shouldn't have told them that, until the age of four, he habitually shat into his father's top hat, preferring this to a cold lavatory seat). This dear man challenged all our cosy preconceptions about children, adolescents and, more painfully, ourselves.

I

He loved children and specialised in child psychology. Sometimes he hurried from our lectures to catch a train, and then a plane to Geneva where he had a part-time job as a consultant with UNESCO. Curiously, he never ever mentioned God to us. His heroes were Jung, Aristotle, and Nye Bevan. And if he mentioned Jesus at all it was Jesus as original thinker rather than spiritual leader.

Tragically, a few years after I had finished the course and was putting his theories into practice, he was charged with sexually abusing the children in his care. He was tried and found not guilty, but during the trial it emerged that his qualifications (an impressive list) were bogus. He hadn't so much as a school-leaving certificate. The Franciscan community swallowed him up and took him into its care and his critics had their hour of triumph. So, my formal education consists of a lacklustre school record and a set of invalidated attendance certificates.

I am told by my graduate friends that I haven't missed much. They go on to describe their last-minute cramming, their worthless thesis (button manufacturing 1797–1831), but they know and I know that, at the very least, they can write a standard essay, they can marshal their thoughts into some sort of order, and they can come up with a reasonable conclusion. Unfortunately I can't do this. I enjoy reading other people's essays (stumbling across Orwell's *Inside the Whale and Other Essays* was a particular teenage joy, it out Elvis'd Elvis), but I can't write a well-structured essay myself. So, in this pamphlet, I have fallen back on the traditional working class method for expressing ideas – the anecdote, or what is now called 'the oral tradition' (which is only a fancy term for working class people talking to each other but not bothering to record what they've heard). I'd better explain that my own background is working class. I use the term easily and unselfconsciously, although I am aware that in 1989 the very words 'working class' are buried in a mine-field over which we all have to tiptoe so very carefully.

Slowly, over the years, our language has been debased, so that terms like 'working class', 'social-ism' and 'the Welfare State' have become pejorative and individuals using the words in conversation now tend to put them in parentheses, either by a certain emphasis of tone or by wiggling the fingers in the air to denote that the speaker is aware of certain ironies – that the words are anachronistic in our technological age.

I am extremely proud of my background and the more I travel and read about history and the roots of what we call civilisation, the prouder I become of this huge international class. I know that they were the builders of the cathedrals, the carvers of the furniture, the seamstresses of the gorgeous clothes in the family portraits. They grew the hot-house flowers, they wove the carpets, bound the books in the libraries and gilded the ceilings. They also built the roads, the railways, the bridges and the viaducts. And what is more they were fully capable of designing such marvels. No one class has a monopoly on vision and imagination. The only thing the working classes lacked was capital.

In the late nineteenth and early twentieth century they lived lives of unrelenting daily grind. They lived in dark unsanitary houses. Their food was tainted, their general health was appalling and the premature death of children and adults was commonplace. Yet these men and women continued to produce vast amounts of wealth for others and enabled this privileged minority to live lives of secure luxury.

There has never been a class-based revolution in England of any lasting significance. When the nearest thing to social revolution came it was in the guise of a series of recommendations, and its author was a titled liberal – Sir William Beveridge.

The modern Welfare State was forged from the white hot metal of the Beveridge Report, particularly the famous 'Three Principles' which were set out in Part One of the report.

It is worth knowing what these three principles were.

FIRST That the wishes of any one section of the community are not given undue weight against any other sections.

SECOND To abolish the 'Five Giants'. Poverty. Disease. Ignorance. Squalor. Idleness.

THIRD To preserve individualism.

Before the bestselling Beveridge Report was published in December 1942, Social Insurance in Great Britain had been pitifully inadequate, there was widespread destitution and millions of working class people who suffered an interruption to their working lives – either through illness or unemployment or other misfortunes – found to their horror that, in exchange for a tiny amount of dole money, they had to give up a proportion of their furniture and clothes. Means-testing officials would decide how many chairs a family needed, and how many saucepans and shirts and clocks and shoes they could do without. In most working class families there is someone who remembers watching as their possessions were taken out of the house and piled into a cart or a lorry – the shame and humiliation felt at the time has not grown any less. A generation of old working class people still distrust and fear officialdom (beware of the Greeks when they come with gifts in their hands): they remember the workhouse, the Means Test Committee, and the pawnshop, not with nostalgia but with anger and justified self-pity.

The Beveridge Report was published six weeks after Alamein, and it took a war to bring about social change. In the words of Karl Marx, 'War is the locomotive of history'. Suddenly working class lads were in demand, never mind that they were malnourished, the army would soon feed them up. And as tens of thousands of these ordinary conscripts died on the battlefields, the army doctors were forced to accept men of an even lower standard of physical fitness. Poverty is not kind to the human body. It is no accident that the rich are healthier and more beautiful than the poor. I have seen some pre-war photographs of working class teenagers. They could be a sub-species of human beings: they are stunted and look almost bestial. Some of the young people are toothless, many have squints and facial deformities, their working clothes are little more than rags, yet they smile into the camera with great delight, thrilled and flattered that somebody should want to take a photograph of *them*: the beasts, who will spend their lives servicing the rich and providing wealth for others, but who will ask for so very little for themselves.

Food rationing at home and army cooks provided

the working classes with a reasonable diet at last. There were noticeable differences in the physical appearance of the next generation of children. They were growing up to be taller and stronger, and they had better teeth and skin. By the time the war ended, the people were more than ready for the Welfare State. They were sick of eating the crumbs off the table – they wanted to pull up a chair and join the feast. The Beveridge Report gave them hope, it recommended the setting up of the Welfare State. Sir William Beveridge was not a socialist and his report was explicitly non-socialist, but it was humanitarian in its recommendations and it came at the right time during a weary war. Most importantly it gave hope to those fighting abroad and those waiting at home that Britain would never be the same again, that destitution and despair would be a thing of the past – to be remembered in the history books but not to be experienced by people in the difficult years ahead.

There were those in the coalition government who opposed the Beveridge Report. To Churchill it was an unnecessary diversion from the war and he was opposed to its implementation. Senior members of the Labour Party – Herbert Morrison, Clement Atlee and Ernest Bevan – took the same line and instructed Labour MPs to vote against it when it was debated in Parliament; but the backbenchers, rallied by Nye Bevan, voted for the report's speedy implementation, and the Welfare State became a reality.

I don't know how old I was when I first saw Aneurin Bevan. All I remember is that I was wearing my school uniform, eating golden syrup sandwiches and reading a book. The lumbering black-and-white television in the corner was turned on, but I paid it no attention. Then onto the screen came the image of Mr Bevan, who was making a speech in a large hall. I was immediately mesmerised – first by his lovely voice, then by his looks. I put my book down and watched as he made a speech. His body dipped and swooped as he started to make a point and then jerked upright to ram the point home. His voice wheedled seductively, dropped until it was only a whisper and then whooshed back up the register, ending in a shouted joke. Because there was so much audience laughter I thought at first that he was a comedian and I half expected him to break into a song and dance routine as comedians did in those days.

When my mother came home from work I asked her about him. 'Oh Nye Bevan, he's a wonderful man. He saved your life when you were a baby.'

For a few years I half believed that Nye Bevan had come to Leicester and had personally administered penicillin to me and cured my pneumonia. I had a pre-pubertal crush on him; when I found out that he was married to Jennie Lee I was tormented with

8

jealousy. I used to watch the television news hoping for a glimpse of him. Very occasionally I was rewarded, he'd usually be in the middle of a gaggle of anonymous Labour politicians who were either going into, or leaving a meeting with fags stuck between their lips.

Eventually Nye's hair turned grey, but this sign of ageing didn't put me off, I thought it added glamour to his potato-faced good looks. By now I was a young adolescent and the passion for social-ism that Nye projected suited my own longing for drama and for absolutes. Socialism also provided a spirituality that I had failed to find during religious assemblies at school or surreptitious visits to out-lying churches where I would sit on a back pew and *will* myself to believe in God. Mr Bevan filled the void left by God perfectly. Because of him I became a socialist and a supporter of the Welfare State. He has been dead for many years and his considerable achievements have now been placed into the wider historical perspective.

It is said that he died a disappointed man due to the failure of the working class to realise its collec-tive strength. Before his death he saw the class that he championed begin to settle for an apathetic materialism, but as one who has her fair share of consumer durables (shopping is my middle name), I would like to tell Mr Bevan that we are only briefly made happy with our new acquisitions. We know there is more to life than our Sony CD. We need to be allowed to express what is great and good in all of us. We need to demonstrate our unselfishness and our love of our fellow human beings. We need our Welfare State, it should free us from crippling insecurity and hardship, it should allow us to soar above the everyday and release the energy and creativity and joy we were born with. From the cradle to the grave.

I am also writing this pamphlet because without the Welfare State and its progeny, the National Health Service, I wouldn't be here. I would have died of pneumonia in my infancy.

I think that's as good a reason as any.

The Quick Birth

I WOKE IN the early hours of the morning on our lumpy second-hand bed. My young husband was asleep next to me. I shook him awake and asked him to go to the telephone. He was still in dreamland and didn't understand at first. I explained that my waters had broken. I was nineteen and had been married for a year and a half.

My husband stumbled into his clothes and ran downstairs and out into the street to the telephone box. I padded myself with a towel and started to gather together the things I would need in the hospital. I worked out that the baby would be seven weeks premature. I began to worry. A condition of our tenancy was 'no children', but I had managed to hide my pregnancy from the landlord when he came for the rent. We had hoped to find another flat in the remaining weeks before the baby was due. What would happen to us when I returned from the hospital with a baby in my arms? I had wanted to look pretty in the hospital and imagined myself wearing broderie anglaise, as I showed off my first child to its proud relations. Instead I packed the lurid nylon nighties that I'd worn during my first year of marriage, bought under the mistaken impression that they were sexy.

My husband returned and we waited for the ambulance together, sitting at the top of the stairs where we could see the front door. The contractions were coming every two minutes. It was a roller-coaster of pain swooping uphill and then gliding down before it began a new ascent.

The ambulancemen were kind and joky as we climbed into the ambulance. How young and frightened we must have looked. When my husband told them that the baby was not due for seven weeks they turned the siren on, cut corners and ignored traffic signals. It was a bumpy ride, and the siren shrieked hysterically as we drove through the matrimonial suburbs towards the hospital. The baby moved inside me; it felt like a graven image as it started its journey to the outside world.

I was pushed towards the labour ward so fast that I banged my elbow on a corner of a wall, and could hear the panting breath of the ambulancemen and my husband who kept up a litany, saying, 'Are you all right?' Then I was in a room so brightly lit that I was momentarily blinded, voices were asking questions, hands removing my clothes. The pain grew. I was shocked by its violence and I shouted out to alert the midwives surrounding me. This couldn't be a normal labour pain, I had read the books, they talked of 'discomfort', not this brutal savagery.

After ten agonising minutes my son was born. He weighed only two pounds and thirteen ounces. A midwife bent down urgently and whispered, 'We are going to christen him now. What do you want to call him?'

'Sean,' I said. I'd been reading Sean O'Casey and my husband was half Irish.

I held Sean for perhaps five seconds. He hadn't cried, half of his body was caved in, and he was smaller than a human being could possibly be. A determined slimmer could lose his weight in a week. The door was violently pushed open by a doctor pulling an incubator behind him. Sean was snatched from me. I heard a choking sound like that of an old man about to spit on a fire, then a wailing cry. My breasts immediately responded to this sound; I felt them fill with milk. Then the incubator was pushed out of the room to be followed by the nurses and doctors. A midwife sat with me as we waited for the afterbirth to come. 'Will he die?' I asked, because I had at last realised the significance of the bedside christening: remembering that somebody had put water on Sean's forehead and said some ritualistic words.

'If he gets through the next few hours he'll have a chance,' she replied. She found it difficult to look me in the eye and I didn't press her for more details. I was shocked by the speed of the birth and exhilarated because the pain had stopped.

Later I was taken to the long ward. I was now clean and smelling of talcum powder and was wearing one of my transparent nighties. I lay inside the tight sheets and blankets of the hospital bed and thought about my son. It was just getting light and I could hear thunder in the distance. The July night had been hot and muggy but this, the first full day of Sean's life, was cool and fresh. Through the high windows I could see trees in the hospital grounds, they were bending in the breeze. Then lightning flashed, illuminating the sleeping women on the ward. Thunder followed, violent and disturbing. Soon the windows were awash with crashing rain. I felt a rush of maternal love for my baby, I wanted to hold him and protect him from the violence of the storm. I wept for him and for myself, because if I knew nothing about babies, how could I be entrusted to look after the tiny boy? It was two days before I was allowed to see him, then when I did, I didn't recognise him. He didn't look like a baby, more like a piece of complicated plumbing. He was yellow, wizened and attached to pipes, some of which were thicker than his fragile limbs. His eyes were open and he seemed to me to be in pain. He was still dangerously ill – only one lung was functioning, he had jaundice and his heart was beating erratically. Time and again the nursing staff brought him back from near death. Somehow, miraculously, he lived.

It is now possible to save babies even smaller than my son, yet such is the state of the National Health Service in 1989 that premature babies are dying because there are not enough incubators to go round. But perhaps even more frightening, small maternity units which serve specific districts are being closed down and sold to property dealers. This will mean that in the future, women will have to travel far greater distances to the larger hospitals. Sometimes taking as much as an hour and a half to complete the journey. This is far too long.

My waters broke at 4.15 am. At 5 am my son was born.

What Katie Does

CHILD BENEFIT is £7.25, this is supposed to pay for all of a child's needs. Let us take an imaginary child and call her Katie. Katie is eleven and attends a comprehensive school. Her father injured his back in an industrial accident and is a semi-invalid, he hasn't worked for three years. Her mother looks after four year old twins. This family is dependant on the state for their income.

But let's concentrate on Katie and how her seven pounds, twenty-five pence a week is spent. She has to eat and the government would like us to eat healthy food, so let's start off by giving Katie a healthy diet.

BREAKFAST
Two Weetabix, eight fluid ounces of milk, orange juice, one piece of wholemeal toast. Cost approx 42p.

LUNCH
Baked potato, tuna fish, an apple, cup of tea. Cost approx 60p.

TEA
Slice of fruit cake, banana. Cost approx 40p.

EVENING MEAL
Two slices of chicken, vegetable rice, salad, glass
of milk. Cost approx 70p.

SUPPER
Two digestive biscuits, cocoa. Cost approx 30p.

The total cost of Katie's *daily* healthy diet comes
to approximately £2.47 (and, as any parent of an
eleven-year-old child will know, I have been very
conservative both with the quantity and the cost of
the food). But on this reckoning poor Katie can
only afford to eat her healthy diet for three days,
and on the fourth day she can only afford to eat
breakfast. Katie will obviously have to eat a less
healthy diet. The fruit will have to go, and the salad,
and she's drinking too much milk. The baked potato
used too much fuel anyway, chips are quicker.
Substitute a beefburger for the chicken. Forget
about the wholemeal bread, white sliced is cheaper.
Does she really need orange juice? That's much
better. Katie's food now costs about one pound
seven pence a day. Katie sits and watches the
television. She eats her beefburger and chips. A
woman comes on the news; she tells Katie that her
chips and white bread are bad for her, she must
change her diet and eat plenty of salads and fruit.
Mrs Currie says that unless Katie does as she is
told she will be a burden on the National Health

Service in years to come. Katie now feels guilty and asks her mother why there is no fruit in the house these days. Her mother says, 'Fruit doesn't grow on trees, it has to be paid for.' But the next day she applies for a cleaning job; cash in hand. 'No names, no pack drill,' says her employer. 'Two pounds an hour, fourteen hours a week.' Another criminal is made. It isn't long before Katie's mother is denounced by a snooper. She is prosecuted and found guilty of fraud. She is now poorer than ever because she has to pay back the amount that the Social Security claim she owes them. She wonders if it is possible to feed a growing child on less than fifty pence a day. She leaves a note for the milkman, 'One pint less until further notice.'

Let us consider other necessities in Katie's life. Clothes, shoes and school equipment. I'll make a list of things that the average school child of Katie's age *needs* in a year. I will be *extremely* mean and will round prices *down*.

2 school skirts	£ 20.00
2 school shirts	£ 17.00
2 school cardigans	£ 24.00
8 prs pants	£ 3.00
2 tee shirts	£ 5.00
2 prs trousers	£ 20.00
2 sweaters	£ 16.00
8 prs socks	£ 6.00

1 denim skirt	£ 12.00
1 denim jacket	£ 15.00
2 prs school shoes	£ 30.00
2 prs trainers	£ 24.00
2 prs plimsolls	£ 12.00
1 school bag	£ 6.00
P.E. skirt (or shorts)	£ 8.00
P.E. top	£ 6.00
Netball skirt	£ 7.00
Leotard	£ 9.00
Track suit	£ 11.00
Pens, pencils, felt tips etc.	£ 6.00
Geometry equipment	£ 3.00
1 anorak	£ 12.00
TOTAL	£272.00

Where will this money come from? Katie is already eating through her family allowance. And her bus fares are £2.00 a week. So far she has no hobbies or interests outside of school. She doesn't go to the cinema or go rollerskating, she does not have swimming, music or dancing lessons. She hasn't had a holiday and her name is not down on the list of children going away with the school next year. She hasn't bought birthday or Christmas cards or small presents for her family. She has not contributed to the charitable appeals at school. She has bought no books and has not replaced her pencils and pens.

Katie's parents are forced into debt.

They borrow £500 from the government's special needs fund, but the repayments cut into their already impossibly low, incoming budget. They panic. They take out a loan with one of the many loan sharks who are waiting to devour the weak and the poor. They intend to pay off the remaining government loan in one payment but there are Katie's shoes to buy and an electricity bill to pay. They are soon caught in a downward spiral of financial despair. Soon this family are receiving expensive professional attention from a doctor, a social worker, a probation officer, a solicitor, a psychiatrist and several policemen. When all they *honestly* ever wanted was something cheaper and simpler – enough money.

Tales Out of School

ONE WET MORNING my sister and I were in a car passing my daughter's junior school. A van drew up in front of us and stopped. We watched as the driver of the van opened the back doors and took out two metal boxes from the inside. He set them down on the pavement on the street side of the school railings, got back into his van and drove off. The rain splashed onto the metal boxes. Within seconds little puddles had formed in the recessed lids. At first we wondered what the boxes were and then we twigged: the school dinners had arrived.

Half an hour later we passed by again, the tins were still out in the rain. We wondered how many dogs had cocked their legs against these inviting territorial markers.

I know what the tins contained because I asked my daughter later that night. Cold chips, cold baked beans, cold beefburgers and doughnuts. Local Education Authorities which were desperately short of funds had found an easy saving. They closed down the school kitchens and sacked most of the dinner ladies. At the same time the government allowed the LEAs to drop their standards of nutrition. The majority of meals for schoolchildren are now prepared in places called Central Kitchens. I use the word 'prepared' because in no sense is the food in these kitchens *cooked* – it is defrosted, reconstituted, and warmed up. The food is then placed into containers which are in turn placed inside the metal boxes. A van picks the boxes up and distributes them to the various schools in the district. The van driver is always in a hurry – he doesn't have time to take the boxes inside the building, so he leaves them outside for the school caretaker to collect.

I'm sure that further rationalisation is possible. Why not issue the children with the plastic sachets of pulpy food that spacemen are forced to eat as they hurtle around the world? There would have to be an initial capital investment on a pair of scissors for use in each of the school dining halls around the land, but think of the convenience, the savings in time and staff wages. No crockery or cutlery would be needed. Snip the corner off the sachet, squirt the contents into the mouth and throw the empty sachet into the bin. The children wouldn't need to sit down, they could eat on the hoof. The tables and chairs in the dining halls would then be redundant and could be sold off at auction. Think of the savings. It makes your mouth water.

The headmaster of my primary and junior school was a Welshman, he was also – I found out only two years ago – a socialist and a passionate supporter of the Welfare State. One, tangible example of his commitment to this great ideal was the school dining hall, and the quality of the food served in it.

It was a pretty room in which to eat: chintz curtains at the windows, the floor was burnished parquet and the trestle tables were covered in gingham cloths. It was a tradition in the school that each table (which seated eight) should be decorated with bowls of flowers, and I had the delightful job of flower monitor. Every morning I was released from a lesson and given twenty minutes to pick flowers and shrubbery from around the school grounds. I would arrange them into the little pots and troughs made by the children in their pottery lesson. Other children laid the tables with table-cloths, metal cutlery, glasses, water jugs and salt and pepper pots. As we worked we became mad-dened by hunger, we could smell food. At the end of the dining hall was the kitchen, a noisy steaming place where the dinner ladies sang and shouted to each other over the rattle of the huge saucepans they wielded. These women were proper cooks and we children ate like little kings and queens: delicious dark brown stews, fluffy cheese pies, huge bowls of salads and dishes full of steaming potatoes. The food always came with a garnish – a sprig of parsley decorated the fish pie, and freshly picked mint was served with the roast lamb. On special occasions like Easter and Christmas the cooks would bake cakes and biscuits and would come out

23

from behind their serving hatches and perambulate the dining hall, showing off their handiwork. At Christmas the curtains would be drawn, the lights turned off, and the cooks would appear at the kitchen door with flaming Christmas puddings and jugs of custard. They had taken off their overalls and were wearing their ordinary clothes and party hats and the headmaster would invite them to sit down with the children, pull a cracker and rest for a while before they tackled the washing up.

I was no good at my schoolwork. In most of my lessons I felt worthless and stupid. I received the most valuable lessons of all in the dinner hall. The flowers on the table exemplified the highest possible standards. It cost so little but it meant so much. It was a gesture of respect from powerful adults to powerless children.

The boxes on the pavement are a gesture of contempt for children and for the whole notion of welfare and the Welfare State.

1975: Gary, Daz and Craig

IT WAS MY precious day off from the Adventure Playground where I worked, so I was not pleased when I looked up from my newspaper to see three of the most difficult teenagers who used the playground come stomping down my garden path. I thought they'd come to cadge money or cigarettes, but I was wrong.

'We're leaving school in three weeks. Can you teach us to read?'

They were sixteen years of age, each of them had received eleven years of compulsory education, and yet not one of those hulking quick-witted lads could read so much as a Cornflakes packet. They could barely write their names and addresses. I asked them to show me what they *could* do, and it took Gary three minutes to write his christian name and surname: he formed each letter with as much concentration as a monk starting a new page of an illuminated manuscript; by the time he'd finished he was sweating and anxious, glad that the arduous task I'd set him was over. I asked them about their schoolwork. 'We don't do none,' was the reply.

'I've sat with the same reading book in front of

me for three years now,' said Craig. I asked him what it was about – this over-familiar book.

'Dunno. Smugglers, I think,' he said laughing.

What had brought about this sudden thirst for literacy was that 'a bloke' had come to the school to inform the school-leavers about such inspiring subjects as how to fill in the forms to apply for state benefits and where to position the address on a letter – should they be keen enough to apply for a job.

The boys said that after the lesson ended they talked to the 'bloke'. They asked what would happen if somebody couldn't read or write and so couldn't fill in a form. According to them, the bloke said that the illiterate person concerned would need to take the form to the appropriate office where an official would complete the form for them. All they would then need to do was to sign at the bottom.

I thought about Gary and his three-minute signature. In my mind's eye I could see the impatient clerk, and hear her sighs of annoyance as the queue built up behind his nervous back.

I questioned them very closely about the secondary school they attended. Though *attended* is hardly the right word – I found out later that the truancy level for their school was abnormally high. On an average day only sixty per cent of the children would be in school. The other forty per cent would be staying in for the gas man, or watching the baby, or shoplifting, or just staying in bed reading comics (those lucky enough to have acquired the special and rare skill of reading).

I asked if anyone on the school staff was actively trying to teach them to read and write. They answered 'No', then one of them said, by way of explanation, 'We're in the dumbo class, see.'

I didn't point out that it was precisely *because* they were in the dumbo class that they needed and were entitled to specialist teaching; they hadn't come to me for an analysis of their problem, they'd come to me for a solution.

I couldn't help them. I'm not a teacher. I'm impatient and disorganised and my domestic and working life at that time was already stretched to fill every waking hour. I telephoned a literacy scheme and gave the boys some details of when the evening classes were held. I also gave them some *Beano* and *Dandy* annuals to take home. None of the boys had a book of any type in the house. All three had chaotic family lives, in which death, divorce and separation had left their mark. All three of them were living in poverty in damp, badly repaired houses on a problem housing estate. This pre-war estate was charmingly known as China-town because of the flickering candlelight to be seen in so many of the houses after dark. However the candlelight did not mean that residents were sitting in their front rooms enjoying romantic dinners for two. It meant that their electricity had been cut off.

Gary, Daz and Craig left my house with their annuals under their arm and their over-optimistic hopes dashed. I had gently broken the news to them that it could take a few years of going to literacy classes before they would be fully literate. And, even as I said the words, I knew they would never go – education to them meant ridicule and humiliation, they couldn't possibly conceive that it could also be enlightening and enjoyable. During our conversation they had told me awful stories about the school. I'll call it Lowood, after *Jane Eyre.*

They had said that the headmaster was mad and violent and given to sudden attacks of rage, when he would burst out of his office, grab the nearest child and attack him with a cane. The boys were surprisingly kind when talking about the headmaster, using expressions like – 'Poor bleeder', and ''Course he can't help himself.'

One of the headmaster's (I'll call him Squeers) latest edicts was that the children were not allowed to talk in the dining hall. Their conversation hurt his ears, he said. I told the boys I'd like to make an appointment to meet Squeers. 'Oh, come anytime,' they said. 'He never does no work.'

I persuaded my colleague Paul to go to the school with me. We were going to invite Squeers to visit our Adventure Playground so that he could see how his pupils spent their spare time. We walked the short distance from the Adventure Playground, passing child truants brazenly walking past the school windows, and went to the main entrance; somebody had painted a huge swastika on the lovely carved doors, the black paint had blistered and it was obvious that the swastika was at least two years old. We rang the bell, the door was opened by a child we knew, who was door monitor that day. He was wearing an anorak and fingerless gloves. 'Squeers has turned the heating off,' he said as he led us through the school. The entrance hall of most schools is usually a delight to the eye, bright with pictures and embroidered hangings and examples of woodwork and metalwork. It's normal to see posters advertising events and giving information. But the entrance hall of Lowood had absolutely nothing on its walls. The corridors were bare too. A few children passed, all wearing their coats and toting plastic carrier bags which contained their school books and sports kit. Our child guide knocked on the headmaster's door, grinned at us, as if to say, 'You'll see!' then scarpered back down the corridor.

We went into the room and into the presence of a madman.

He was small and wiry and as dapper as a bookie's runner. His thinning hair was stuck to his scalp with Brylcreem. Before we could introduce ourselves he came out from behind his desk – which was raised on a dias – and began to shadow-box with my astonished colleague, Paul. He also began a monologue which was not to stop until Paul and I fled, two hours later. He talked about his unsatisfactory sex life – he blamed his wife. He said how lovely it was to have little girls in his school at last, after teaching boys for thirty years. 'I encourage gymnastic displays,' he said. 'I like to see the little girls in their leotards.' He talked about his amateur boxing career. 'The boys know I can knock them out with one punch. I have no problems with discipline.' (Not true; at frequent intervals he would run out of his office and scream at some hapless group of children to no effect at all – they simply carried on doing whatever they were doing before he interrupted them.)

He demonstrated his collection of canes, taking them from the wall behind his desk where they hung in order of size. He explained at mind-numbing length the history of each cane and the pain it was capable of inflicting, and said that the cane was a marvellous deterrent. Then he showed us the Punishment Book, in which the same names appeared over and over again. He was sorry to say that he'd been forced to cane some of the naughty girls, their parents had been up to the school to complain – good job he could handle himself; some of the mothers had been quite violent. He explained that he was having staffing difficulties – teachers left suddenly, giving no reason. 'No backbone!' He said that most of the children in his school were mongrels – the results of in-breeding. Did we know that there had been two public meetings called by parents to protest at the low standards of his school? It wasn't his fault if the children were too thick to pass exams, was it? Even the community policeman had spoken out against him at one meeting.

'I run a tight ship,' he said. 'That's why they want to get rid of me.' His Deputy Head came into the office, a distraught young man who could have been fresh from Teacher Training College. There was trouble in the woodwork room.

Squeers said, 'Can't you see I have visitors?'

I squirmed in my chair and shortly afterwards we left, bothered and bewildered but far from bewitched. Then, in the manner of survivors of a major accident, Paul and I began to talk about what we'd experienced. We compared notes – had Squeers really said that the children were mongrels? Had he really got up and shadow-boxed around his office? I was glad I had Paul as a witness, for without him I may have thought I was hallucinating. How was it possible for such a deranged person to be in charge of the education of thousands of children over the years? The illiteracy level of children leaving that school was one of the highest in the country, and it was tolerated only because the school was in the middle of a poor working class area; nobody expected the children to do well. There were only so many places at sixth form college and university. What would happen to the structure of higher education if it was to be flooded with eager candidates from areas like Chinatown? Let nobody think for a moment that the children did not have the capability. I got to know hundreds of them on the Playground, and they were as intelligent as any children I've met anywhere in England (with the possible exception of Liverpool). It was unfortunate for them that many of their parents had been to the same or a similar school. One day, after a tip-off, a newly elected county councillor 'happened' to drop in to see Squeers and he was given the full, mad routine. The councillor was horrified and reported back to County Hall. Not long afterwards Squeers retired, Lowood School was considered to be beyond reclamation and was closed down and the children were sent to other schools in the neighbourhood. Gary, Craig and Daz are all married now; they have children of their own. I sometimes see them in the town. Those boys may not have set the world on fire; but at least they have all made sure that their children can read.

Every year there are hundreds of thousands of children in Britain who leave our schools unable to read and write properly. I do not think that there are many among them who attended a public school or were privately educated. Money is involved, big money. The vast majority of our young illiterates attended state comprehensive schools, *compulsorily attended.* It's the law of the land that children must receive an education. Try keeping your child away from school and see what happens. You will be taken to court and fined. When the state *fails* to educate a child, there are no repercussions. I look forward to the day when the parents of an illiterate child – that is, a child who has been badly taught – take the state to court and win substantial damages. Perhaps then standards of literacy will rise and we can all enjoy the benefits of a more literate population. It's bad enough that most of us in Britain do not know a second language. Not to be able to read and write your first language after eleven compulsory years at school is scandalous and unforgiveable.

Taking The Bottles Back

'IF THE CONDUCTOR asks how old you are, tell him you're four,' I instructed my five-year-old son. We were waiting at the bus stop. All I had in my purse was eleven pence. Enough for my fare into town but not for his half-fare.

Throughout the journey he asked in a voice that could cut through limestone, 'Am I four or five?'

'Four' I mumbled, looking at the conductor. We were on our way to the Town Hall. Our party consisted of me, the five-year-old boy, the two-year-old boy and my baby daughter. For a treat we sat upstairs on the bus. When we passed Leicester prison my eldest son shouted, 'Daddy lives there, doesn't he, Mummy?' His podgy finger pointed at the forbidding building. I was now tired of this family joke. My ex-husband was not and has never been in prison, but naturally the other passengers on the bus were not to know this.

The five-year-old is now twenty-four and has (in my opinion) an unhealthy obsession with Kafka. I blame this on his earlier, obsessive interest in Leicester prison – which looks like a sinister Ruritanian castle.

The four of us were on our way to collect our

weekly maintenance. I was expecting nine pounds. It wasn't there. The woman behind the grille looked through a large ledger.

'No,' she said. 'No money has been paid in.'

I didn't know what to do. I asked her advice.

'You must go to the Social Security office,' she said. She gave me the address. I ran across the town pushing the little ones in the push-chair and urging the five-year-old to pretend he was in a running race. We got there at about a quarter to four. The office was up three flights of filthy stairs. The lift was out of order. Precious time passed getting the children up the stairs. We were given a number and told to wait. It was an awful room: the walls and the seats were institutional orange, the floor consisted of fag holes, and there were no ashtrays, although most of the claimants were smoking. The receptionist sat behind a glass screen. I had to bellow to be heard.

'I've got no money.'

I gave my name and address. She frowned. 'You're in the wrong office.'

The office I wanted was on the other side of town, it closed at 5.30. It was now five o'clock, the children were hungry, the baby was crying. I was near to tears myself. We reached the other office at 5.20 pm. This new waiting-room was worse than the earlier one. It was an older building and was the one where the winos and tramps were registered.

There was an air of panic in the room, and a pool of vomit in the corner. I had ten minutes in which to state my case and leave – with money in my pocket. I needed the bus fare and money to buy food. As before, I was given a number and told to wait. I explained I couldn't wait, I needed 50p in cash. An emergency payment.

'We'll send it to you,' I was told.

'When?'

'In a few days, when we've looked into your case. We need your birth certificate, marriage certificate, and a copy of your legal separation documents.'

I agreed to bring these documents in the next day. But in the meantime I had no bus fare – how would I get home, and, how would I feed my children?

'Haven't you got any relatives who'll lend you some money?' said the young man behind the desk.

It is impossible to convey to somebody who has money and no children the nightmare of having children and no money. I knew nobody who was on the telephone at that time. I couldn't even reverse the charges and ask for help.

I couldn't face walking the five miles home. I begged the young man for 50p, but he wouldn't relent. The staff in the back office started to put their coats on and tidy their desks. Half-past five arrived. Most of the people in the waiting-room were ushered out. Others, desperate like me, stayed – explaining – some in tears, others shouting, that they hadn't eaten, had nowhere to stay. It was bedlam. My children were hot and thirsty. Could I give them a glass of water?

'No,' the office was now closed.

'You lend me 50p – as a person, you'll get it back,' I said.

'No,' he said. 'Where would it end if I started to do that?'

I wanted to tell him that I was a literate and intelligent person, not just the young mother of these crying children – for Christ's sake I had read every page of *War and Peace*. When I could afford it I read the *Guardian*. I was a Bessie Smith fan. I had won several prizes for verse speaking. I could read a menu in French. A poet had been in love with me. I knew how to spell and pronounce Dostoevsky. I had worked hard since I was fifteen. I had paid my taxes and my national insurance. I had never broken the law and all I wanted from the Welfare State was a stinking lousy sodding 50p.

I didn't get it.

It is a terrible thing to see your mother crying. I tried very hard, I contorted my face this way and that but eventually, when we were out on the street, the tears came. The four of us walked along – a quartet of cry-babies.

I was too proud to stop passers-by and ask for

help. I scanned the pavements looking for money. Instead I found lemonade bottles, 'Corona' brand. There was a returnable deposit of 4p on each bottle.

My eldest son cheered up, he knew that these bottles represented hard cash. My pride vanished, I looked in litter bins, I looked over walls and behind fences. Soon we had enough for my bus fare, and then we had enough for four ice lollies – don't anybody dare to even *think* that those children should have been given something *healthy* to eat.

When we got home I bathed the children, and, when they were clean and shining in their pyjamas, I said we were going to have a special treat for dinner. I emptied the food cupboard of its contents. It didn't take long. There was a packet of beef suet, a tin of golden syrup, a tin of peas and one Oxo cube. For dinner we had pea soup (put another pea in the soup, Mother) and golden roly-poly. My eldest child still remembers this meal. We laid a tablecloth on the living room floor and ate in picnic fashion. Late that night I put a note out for the milkman asking him to leave bread, butter and eggs, and in the morning our breakfast was waiting on the doorstep. Milkmen are a good source of credit. God bless them every one.

Later that day I rang the Town Hall. There was still no money so I went back to the Social Security Office. My family lent me five pounds. My friend looked after the children. I took my documents, but most important of all I put a copy of that day's *Guardian* on the counter between me and the young counter clerk. He talked to me with considerably more respect than he had done the day before. A fat lot of good it did me; my Social Security payment took nine days to arrive, but by then I had taken three part-time jobs and employed two young girls as baby-sitters, and the system had beaten me. I became a working mother.

I would like to report that the DSS conducts itself with more humanity today, but I can't because it doesn't.

In early January 1989 I read a report in the local paper. It said that a man had gone berserk in a DSS office. He'd broken the office Christmas tree and stamped on the glass baubles. My second son was in the waiting-room with a friend, he'd already told me about this unhappy scene. Apparently the man had been waiting two weeks for a promised Giro. He was married with children, he'd been sacked from his job as a hosiery mechanic and like all sacked people, he was refused dole. He was desperate for money, it was two days before Christmas. The counter staff told him it was in the Christmas post; they had been telling him this for eight days. The man had tried telephoning but the DSS phone lines were permanently engaged. Finally, in high bad temper, knowing there were only two shopping days before Christmas, he

39

had got on a bus and come in person for his money.

In court he was described as being 'of previous good character'. But in the DSS office he turned into Mr Jekyll, he started to shout. The police were sent for. When they arrived he tried to explain his case. They wouldn't listen, they started to push him out. He refused to leave without his money, they pushed harder. The Christmas tree was knocked over, the man then stumbled and fell amongst the glass baubles which had fallen with the tree. Soon wild confusion reigned, the man, the policeman, the DSS staff and a few disgruntled DSS petitioners fought amongst the pine needles. Quite soon the man was overcome, arrested, and taken to the police station.

He was charged with assaulting the police, resisting arrest, and criminal damage to a Christmas tree and decorations.

It would be funny if it wasn't so tragic.

I don't know how much it cost the state to prosecute the poor man and lock him up and sentence him, but I'm sure, absolutely positive, that it would have cost at least a hundred times more than his paltry, delayed, Giro.

The DSS offices are not given enough funding, their staff are poorly paid and are driven to distraction by the amount of work they have to do. The regulations which govern their decisions are incredibly complicated. There is frequent turnover of staff. Morale is extremely low. Working with desperate people all day (on both sides of the counter) is very dispiriting; their unhappiness rubs off on you. For the sake of self-preservation you develop a thicker skin, you come to regard the claimants as the enemy. Because they are inarticulate in the presence of articulate officialdom, you do not respect them and habitually talk to them as though they are of lower intelligence than yourself. You are frightened of them, and all your communication takes place behind a glass screen. The furniture they sit on is screwed down because, in the past, this furniture has been thrown *at* you. They offend you in their poverty, you despise their clothes and shoes. Some of them smell and have disgusting personal habits. That is why it is impossible to allow them free access to the lavatory; why they must queue up and ask for the key. They question your decisions. You know that most of these disputes when taken in front of a tribunal are won by the claimants. You work in dingy and sometimes sordid surroundings, there is very little – apart from the babies and children in the waiting-room – to delight the eye. But you are tired of the children, and don't give them a second glance after a while. You've been on strike – not just for better pay and conditions for yourself, but for a better deal for the claimants. So you are not without hope of redemption. You feel helpless in the face of such massive bureaucratic machinery. You are forced to rush each interview, to appear detached, as the painful circumstances are related to you – death, dismissal, separation, divorce, chronic illness.

Nobody goes to a DSS office to ask for state benefits if they are well and happy and employed. Nobody needs to. There is no need to have vile surroundings and seemingly uncaring staff as a disincentive. People down on their luck deserve the best: beautiful surroundings and well-paid professional staff to help them out of their difficulties.

Why not train thousands more social workers and let them sit in on claimants' interviews? Most social problems could be helped or prevented if people had more money and practical advice. The present benefits system is unfair, inefficient, and totally unprofessional; which is why millions of people do not claim the benefits to which they are legally entitled. There is hysterical emphasis today on preventing the abuse of the system by a tiny proportion of fraudsters (known as scroungers). But the abuse lies elsewhere; in the Department of Social Security. They do not aid their staff or their clients' health, and they undermine *everyone's* security.

Monitoring the Heart

I WAS SITTING up in my hospital bed in a cardiac unit which was housed in a sort of Nissen hut. I was eating an orange and reading a newspaper. A headline caught my eye: 'Mole Mum Fights for Life'. I immediately started to feel ill. My first reaction on seeing anything in a newspaper is to believe what I read. My second reaction is to disbelieve every last comma.

I was in the Nissen hut because two days before I had been taken ill with what was described to me as 'Not quite a heart attack'. I'd been preparing for my youngest daughter's birthday party and was crossing the hall with a plate of cling film and cake when my eldest daughter laughed and asked, 'Mum, why are you walking like a crab?'

I explained that I'd got a pain in my chest and went on my crab-like way to lay the table. I scuttled around for a few more minutes and then urged by my alarmed daughter I telephoned my diabetic consultant (all insulin junkies like me are given their doctor's home telephone number). It was Sunday morning and he told me he was frying a pan of bubble and squeak. I described my symptoms, pain in chest for six weeks – but now walking in a crouch.

He turned off his bubble and squeak and arranged to meet me at the local casualty department. I rang for a taxi and left my daughters at home to contact relations and ask for their help with the party guests who would be on their way.

The casualty department was busy, and there was a queue at the desk which I joined like a good Englishwoman. The pains in my chest intensified. I tried to remember if I was wearing sensible or frivolous underwear. I knew that within a few minutes all would be revealed. I wished that I'd shaved my legs. I also wished that my husband wasn't on a mountain in the north of Scotland. My doctor arrived looking unfamiliar in his Sunday morning clothes, and took me into a side room where he hooked me up to an electro-cardiograph machine. There was trouble at t'mill. A lockout. The blood couldn't easily get into the heart. There was an obstruction of some kind. I was wheeled into Intensive Care, more of my frivolous underwear was revealed, I began to feel peculiar and for a split second I thought I was going to die, and then I began to worry about the birthday party: ten little girls were supposed to be taken to the circus in half an hour's time, what was happening at home? My kind diabetic doctor offered to go back to my house and see what was happening. Before he left he took hold of my hand and squeezed it – was this the long farewell? A nurse put a name tag on my wrist. 'Sue

Townsend,' she said aloud. 'How embarrassing to have the same name as that woman who writes those silly books.' I kept quiet.

People were working all over my body. I felt like a luxury car being serviced. I wanted to pass my MOT and take to the road. The young Asian doctor who seemed to be in charge told me that I was 'very young to be having a heart attack'. So this is what it's like to have a heart attack, I thought. No clasping of the throat and dramatic staggering around before falling on the floor, more a sliding into helplessness and then a murky, confused leaving behind of your body. It was the ordinariness of it all that was so strange. I certainly didn't fight for my life, but neither was I particularly pacifistic.

I got it into my head that I mustn't go to sleep, and so I forced my eyes open and watched the doctors and nurses as they worked. I left the casualty department attached to drips and monitors and was taken upstairs to the cardiac unit where I was put in a darkened room. For once in my life I didn't feel like reading. A beautiful West Indian sister let in a visitor – it was my diabetic doctor. All the party guests had turned up and were having a good time, he said. (Later when I got home from the hospital I asked my daughter if she'd enjoyed the circus. 'No,' she replied, 'it was horrible, they tortured the animals.')

At midnight I was told I was being transferred to

another hospital where I was going to have an operation called a cardioangioplasty. The ambulance stopped outside a Nissen hut, and my diabetic doctor, who had driven ahead, was waiting at the door. He explained that a team of doctors and nurses were being gathered together.

My family came to see me; they were pale and frightened. They'd had an eventful day. My niece had hit her head on the pole which held up the big top at the circus. While I'd been upstairs in my dark room, she had been downstairs having stitches in her head. 'We're certainly getting our whack out of the National Health Service today,' somebody said, it could have been me.

It was the first time the medical team had worked together in the middle of the night and on a patient who hadn't made an appointment. There was a very jolly atmosphere in the operating theatre. The surgeon explained to me what was about to happen. A catheter would be introduced into the artery in my groin, and it would then be manipulated until it reached a blocked artery of the heart. Once there, a small balloon would be blown up and the gunge causing the blockage would be eroded. I would only need a local anaesthetic, so if I fancied it I could watch the operation on a television monitor.

It should have won a BAFTA award, it was riveting stuff. My diabetic doctor played the romantic male lead, I of course was the female lead, and the surgeon was the hero. But nobody got the girl in the end, not even death.

In the early hours of the morning I was taken to the Intensive Care Unit, where I lay awake and watched the heart monitor. Two more patients were brought in during the early hours, both elderly men. I could hear their womenfolk talking to them from behind the thin curtains that separated our beds. All three of us received constant supervision from a sister and a nurse. Each of us were attached to heart monitors. What I didn't know at the time was that these monitors were practically the only working monitors in the whole of the cardiac unit, which had thirty or so patients. The hospital was so short of money that they couldn't afford new monitors and couldn't afford to repair the old ones. To add to this unhappy situation, there were not enough skilled technicians available to maintain or repair the existing machines. I was given a monitor because I was young and had a family. The old men had one each because nobody younger than them came in that night.

This unit was also short of cotton wool and disposable gloves. Nurses would steal away under cover of darkness and borrow these basic necessities from other, more prosperous wards. They spent a lot of time discussing amongst themselves how to acquire the equipment they needed to do their jobs. They were scandalised by the situation, but helpless to effect a change. Government cuts to the National Health Service had bled them dry. They were now in the invidious position of *choosing* who to help live, when they wanted so desperately to help all their patients to live for as long as possible.

The National Health Service was founded by decent people who valued human life and happiness. Their intention was to provide patients with free health care at the point of need. They could not have envisaged that in the late 1980s patients were being forced to pay after all; with their lives.

Community Care

A NORTH-EAST wind was blowing down London Road in Leicester. Office workers walked in hunched groups to join the queues shivering outside the lunchtime sandwich shops. Amongst them walking gracefully on the cold pavement was a barefoot black girl.

She was naked apart from a tiny skirt made of dried grass which had been coloured bottle green. Her hair was arranged in matted dreadlocks and fell to the small of her back. She was a female Friday to a non-existent Robinson Crusoe. She was tall and had a beautiful body with well-shaped breasts and legs; but her face lacked expression and her lips were moving although she had no companion. Naturally she caused a sensation as she progressed up the road, she was surrounded by laughter and shocked comment. She looked the same age as my eldest daughter, nineteen, and I wanted to leap out of the car I was in and cover her from the wind and protect her from the gawping men who were having such fun at her expense. But I didn't, and neither did anyone else. Soon she was out of sight, but I couldn't forget her.

They call it a city but Leicester is really a village. I

asked about the black girl, many people knew of her. She'd been seen in shops and supermarkets dressed (or rather undressed) in the same extraordinary manner. My daughter had seen her standing on a corner dressed only in a man's vest. She had stood without moving 'like a statue' for half an hour. People had approached her in a kindly manner and asked if she needed help, but she had not responded in any way. Others had approached her with less kindness. She lived in a community care hostel. She had joined the ranks of the street entertainers: the mad, the eccentric, and the mentally ill who are discharged from our hospitals and into the care of our embarrassed and indifferent community. She and others had become court jesters to the passing public. Unpaid and ill-rehearsed they roam the streets, they are the vagabonds of the shopping precincts, acting out their obsessions and fantasies to an amused public. Most people smile when they see them. Their real names become lost. The public rename them.

Everyone in Leicester knows Panda Mary. I first saw her in a pizza parlour, and she was carrying five soft toys in her arms. One, a huge black and white panda, had given her her nickname. Mary stinks of stale urine; she, and her clothes, are filthy, and it is impossible to guess her age. She could be thirty-five, she could be fifty-five; hard times and weather have not been kind to her face.

It is Mary's fancy to kiss shop assistants and

waitresses. She will rush into an establishment and shout in a very loud voice, 'Where's my friend?' People will cower away but she is very persistent and will hunt somebody down and smother their face with kisses. The soft toys are in a constant state of movement. They are dropped, shifted from one arm to the other, sometimes they ride in plastic carrier bags – their heads poking out of the top. The big panda is too big to put into a bag, this grimy beast is slung over Mary's shoulder when, at the end of the day, she and her other furry friends make their way back to their hostel.

Mary is tolerated by most establishments; to my knowledge only McDonalds have banned her. I saw Mary last week, when she was without her stuffed companions. She sat on a bench in the city centre. She looked miserable cold and drugged.

There is another well-known street entertainer called the Happy Man, he stands on a busy corner directing the traffic with a pole trimmed with feathers. He wears a permanent smile and sings to himself. His clothes and his hat are covered – smothered – in badges and other pretty adornments. He looks like an exotic bird and he even has a beak-like nose. He does no harm and receives none. The last time I saw him he had plastic bags tied around his shoes and he had decorated his trouser turn-ups with garlands of plastic flowers. He looked like a superannuated Morris dancer on May morning.

His happiness keeps him from harm; it is an invisible shield – a protection. He is the town talisman; see him and you'll be lucky. And, when the traffic lights break down his feathered stick comes into its own. For a few minutes – before the grim-faced uniformed authorities arrive – the Happy Man takes over, he controls the traffic and perhaps, for a few glorious minutes, he *is* cared for by the community.

I was once a member of a juvenile acting company called 'The Orpheans', and we (perhaps foolishly) took our Passion play about the life of Jesus to several grim mental hospitals. Once we went to a place called Carlton Hayes, a huge Victorian institution near Leicester. From my vantage point on the cross – I starred as Jesus – I could see the audience very clearly, they cackled and slobbered and cried out, they wore ill-matched clothes and peculiar shoes. Their hair was cut in brutal shapes, old ladies sported full beards. There were men in the audience who were more interested in their genitals than 'The Orpheans'.

Earlier, when I had dragged my cross up the aisle, several patients had left their seats to help me out. One man had a violent reaction and had to be dragged away. It was quite difficult to act out holiness in these circumstances, but the show went on. When the nails were hammered into my palms many patients started to sob in genuine anguish. People began to demand that I be let down from the cross. Before long the audience was on its feet distressed and frightened. They only calmed down when I was resurrected and appeared in my nice white robes and walked down the aisle smiling and blessing them, and promising them eternal life.

Later, when I had returned to my dumpy atheistic self, our group was invited to take tea. We were led down the long corridors past locked wards from where shrieks and screams could be heard. We passed patients exhibiting strange behaviour and through the windows we glimpsed groups of patients gardening apathetically. We took a short cut through a ward and saw the crammed in beds and lockers. We passed the dayroom where people sat around day after endless day.

We didn't linger over our tea and I was glad when we got into our coach and left the hospital grounds. I felt that I had glimpsed hell. I was determined *never* to have a nervous breakdown.

Unfortunately, in 1980, a friend of mine did break down. One evening without warning she started to behave in a very bizarre and alarming manner. She ran into the auditorium of a theatre and interrupted the performance by shouting abuse at the actors on stage. She then left and sat at a table in the theatre bar singing to herself. Later she walked into heavy traffic and was almost knocked over by a lorry. During the night her behaviour deteriorated. She made several determined efforts to kill herself. Her friends guarded the doors and windows, she found a knife and used it to fend us off while she phoned members of her family, and, to their astonishment (because she'd always been placid and gentle), she abused them and accused them of committing sexual perversions.

When the doctor arrived she became her normal self and we, the friends, were accused by the doctor of hysterical over-reaction. The moment the door shut behind the doctor she went berserk. We telephoned the doctor again, he refused to return. We called an ambulance. When the ambulancemen arrived they found my friend sitting with her legs dangling over the edge of the windowsill. She was serenading the street, with an eerie, made-up song about her life. The ambulancemen watched her for half an hour before calling another doctor. This doctor confirmed that she had suffered a nervous breakdown, another doctor was called and she was committed to hospital. Then, with great skill and patience, the ambulancemen persuaded her to get into the ambulance. She insisted that all the windows in the vehicle be opened, and, as we drove out of town she fluttered her fingers in the dawn breeze. She was taken to a mental hospital, the place of my childhood nightmare. When she had been put to bed, I went to say goodbye. As I bent down to kiss her she turned away from me and said she would never forgive me for 'putting her away'. But I was happy to leave her there, as she needed care and four secure walls.

I went to visit her a few weeks later. She told me that the nurses were poisoning her. She wanted me to post a letter to the police. We walked in the lovely gardens and then sat in a summer-house while she explained that God had spoken to her and told her she was wicked and had to be punished. She then told me that she hated me and asked me not to visit her again.

The last I heard of her was that she was out of hospital and was a member of a fundamentalist Christian group. She and other converts hold open-air meetings where they harangue the public. My friend sings hymns in her beautiful voice with the help of a cheap tape-recorder – I expect she attracts a lot of attention because she has an exquisite face and an elegant, dancer's body. I don't know if she has told the earnest young men she prays with that she once worked in Paris as a dancer, or that her working costume consisted of sequins and stilettos and very little else. The hospital had changed dramatically since my last visit as Jesus. The introduction of new drugs meant that patients were more manageable – giving both them and the staff more freedom of movement; and there was an emphasis on therapy, allowing patients a chance to talk for the first time about things that had bothered them all their lives.

In 1989 the hospital and its grounds are under

threat, as a property company want to build an estate of executive houses in the grounds. They want to convert the old buildings into offices and flats. Millions of pounds are involved. The property speculators point to a major new development in mental health provision: that of treating patients in the community. They argue that the antiquated buildings called insane asylums by the Victorians are redundant now that most patients are controlled by drugs and can live with their families or in the care of the community. If only this were true. I have never met anyone who was happy to have a mentally ill person living with them, however much they may love them, and, despite asking and searching, I have yet to find the community that is prepared to help and care for the recovering mentally ill. There will always be saintly individuals and voluntary groups who do wonderful unrecognised work with the mentally ill, but the larger community? Forget it. They get up petitions *against* hostels. They do *not* care. The ex-patients, the unofficial street entertainers of 1989, need protecting *against* the community.

We still need the buildings and the trees and the lawns and flowerbeds for those people who cannot yet cope with life outside. Panda Mary can cope – just. The Happy Man copes. But if the beautiful black girl needs to walk near naked and barefoot she should be allowed to do so – in the grounds of a hospital. She is too vulnerable, too young, and too exposed to be walking alone on the community's cold pavements.

The Fiddler on the Train

'GUESS WHAT I've got in my bag,' said the big old man. We were sitting opposite each other on the train, and we were on our way to Leicester. Earlier he had placed four cans of beer on the table – he was already quite drunk but was exuding happiness and goodwill. His voice boomed around the carriage, and there were disapproving looks. One woman, dressed in white to show off her new tan, moved to a different seat after the happy old man offered a swig from his can.

'A snob,' he told me, as she gathered up her duty free bags. 'Go on, guess,' he repeated.

I looked hard at his plastic carrier bag, and he allowed me to feel the weight. It was heavy. I guessed potatoes, bags of sugar, more cans of beer. With each guess he laughed, 'No, no, not in a million years.' He was right.

It was a pig's head. The old man held it up by its ears. Its piggy eyes were open and staring at me accusingly; as if I'd been the one who had parted it from its shoulders.

'I butchered it this afternoon,' he said. My fellow passengers looked on in horror, what would the mad old bugger do next?

Next he brought out a set of gleaming cook's knives. They were individually wrapped in soft cotton and then in thick, impenetrable, canvas.

'The tools of my trade,' he said. 'I was a butcher on the *Queen Mary*.'

He polished his knives with the cloth until they gleamed, then he invited me to test the cutting edges. I obligingly held up a piece of script I'd been working on and he deftly sliced it in half – the quickest editing job I've ever had. I told him that I was impressed and he was pleased. I think everyone, especially the woman in white, was relieved when he stopped waving his knives about and put them away. He sang a few choruses of 'I'll walk beside you', then, ignoring the fact that I was writing, he began to talk to me. This is what he told me as near as I can remember.

'I've been to Hastings today to see my friend who's a butcher. He's an old-fashioned sort who still does his own slaughtering. His slaughterhouse has got a separate address which has proved very handy for me, because I'm fiddling the social and that's where they send my Giro once a fortnight. I got a pensioner's bungalow in Leicester and I get a Giro sent there an' all. And I've got a friend who keeps a boarding house in Yarmouth, so I'm registered there. I'm what is known as a Social Security Scrounger, and I'm not ashamed of it neither. I spent two weeks in a lifeboat during the war, and the rest of the time waiting to be burnt alive in the galley of a destroyer. I'll be dead soon because my liver's gone and I drink too much, but I'm not going to die poor. All I'm doing is claiming the allowances that other old people *should* be claiming. I know at least four old ladies who are too proud to take any extra money from the Social Security, so I take it for them. I like travelling around between the three places. It doesn't cost me much because I've got a pensioners' rail pass. I'm very keen on women and I'm able to take them out and about for a meal, pictures, ballroom dancing, to the races. I live a very happy life, but if I didn't fiddle I'd be a miserable old sod. Sitting in my bungalow, cold and scraping the pennies together for a bite to eat. I expect I'll be caught one day, but they won't send me to prison, will they? I'm seventy-six and I don't care if my picture gets in the papers, I've got no family to shame.'

He hadn't modulated his voice during the telling of his story and I sensed that most of the people in the carriage were quietly enraged. I was astonished at his boldness; for all he knew a Social Security official could be within earshot, the police could be pounding on the door of his bungalow the very next morning.

He followed me off the train and asked me if I wanted to come back to his pensioner's bungalow for a nightcap. (It's years since I had a proposition from anyone under sixty.) I refused, and then, before I could stop him, he had given my taxi driver a five pound note and instructed him to 'take this lady wherever she wants to go.'

I chose to go home. It was a quarter to two in the morning. He carried the pig's head and the knives into the following taxi and our cars drove away, one behind the other. He blew kisses to me through the windscreen and then my taxi turned a corner and the criminal was gone.

I like to think about him and the old ladies spending his ill-gotten gains on sensual pleasures. Perhaps his extra income keeps him and his friends out of expensive geriatric institutions – who knows? It may be that he is *saving* the state money.

The Paupers' Funerals

'I DAREN'T GO by the windows, I can't even draw the curtains.' She was standing in the middle of the living room of her flat. We were nineteen storeys high. I was so breathless that I could hardly speak. I had climbed the concrete stairs because *I* was afraid of the coffin-like lift.

It was 1978. I was the community worker come to call. She was the old lady who needed her windows cleaning. It was the first day of my new job and she was my first 'client'. I took a bottle of Windowlene out of my briefcase (the briefcase gave me confidence) and cleaned the swing windows inside and out. It was no use explaining to the old lady that household cleaning was not included in my job description – that I was supposed to contact the relevant statutory or voluntary agency for practical help. It was quicker and more satisfying to do it myself. I actually enjoyed cleaning two years of grime away from those windows, though I didn't enjoy the unmasking of the terrifying dizzy view.

Her name was Mrs Bradshaw and she had been moved out of her tiny terraced house where she'd lived all her married life into Marston House – twenty-three storeys high and containing 192 flats.

She had not wanted to move, she didn't want to leave the small back garden or the neighbours who had become closer to her than her own family. When she was told by 'them' – the council – that her house would be demolished and that she would be rehoused in Marston House, she had cried herself to sleep every night. She was terrified of heights and she hated lifts. She told me that she screwed up her courage and wrote a letter to the Housing Department asking if she could have a flat on the ground floor. She received a reply saying that the ground floor flats had been allocated to disabled tenants. She felt ashamed then and didn't like to make a fuss, so she let things happen and moved into her flat.

Mrs Bradshaw had one son, Tony. He lived three miles away but she had not seen him for seven years. There had been a silly quarrel one Christmas Day, 'He'd had a drink, we had words, I went to see him on Boxing Day to apologise but he shut the door on me.'

Her cupboards were full of birthday and Christmas presents she'd bought for Tony, his wife and her two grandchildren over the following seven years. Mildewed Easter eggs were stacked in the sideboard and sticks of seaside rock, gone sticky with time, were ranged on the top of her formica kitchen cupboards.

If she went anywhere with the Evergreen Club

she bought Tony and his family a memento, but they never called to be given their presents. There was a photograph of Tony and his family on top of the television. He looked smug and powerful, his wife had prominent teeth. I loathed them on sight. The children were very young – one was a baby. Mrs Bradshaw would not recognise her own grand-children if they called without notice.

She had other problems. The flat stank of stale and fresh urine, her mattress was sodden. She was an incontinent Miss Havisham. She could hardly walk because she could no longer cut her toenails – which were now so hard and bent that they were digging into the underside of her toes. But above all she had recently found out that the funeral policy that she'd been paying into for thirty years would not cover the cost of the decent burial she'd planned. Its encashment value was only sixty pounds and she couldn't possibly put Tony to any expense, could she? He had his wife and kiddies to think about. The proposition she put to me was this – would I arrange to sell her dead body? She'd heard that it was possible. Universities and medical schools were crying out for corpses to practice on, and, when they'd finished practicing they gave your bits and pieces a Christian burial and it didn't cost a penny.

It was my first day in my new job, and Mrs Bradshaw had presented me with enough work to

last me a fortnight. There were 191 other flats to
visit in Marston House and I had not even stepped
foot inside its sister tower block, which loomed in
the near distance, and was also my responsibility. I
promised to help Mrs Bradshaw with her incontinence and her toenails and I said I would enquire
about the sale of her body. I was tempted to track
Tony down and thump him on his smug nose, but
I resisted the temptation. I needed this job. I had
three small children to keep.

The incontinence was helped with incontinence
pads and a bubble sheet from the Red Cross (my
mother worked there). The toenails were displayed
to a horrified Health Visitor who made the earliest
chiropodist appointment possible (six weeks).

The selling of her body proved to be more difficult. 'Had Mrs Bradshaw a rare disease?' I was
asked.

'No,' I replied. 'Sorry then, we're not interested,
we have more than enough geriatric corpses, and
unless there is something *very* unusual about the
manner of dying or the skeletal structure . . .' Feel-
ing increasingly ghoul-like I rang every medical
school in the book. Nobody wanted Mrs Bradshaw's
dead body. Eventually I began to dread seeing Mrs
Bradshaw's *live* body.

'Have you sold it yet?' she would ask each time
I visited. I began to feel like a failed Burke or
Hare. She became irritated with me, her demands

increased. The tenant in the upstairs flat danced all night and kept her awake. Her curtains needed washing, would I fetch her pension and her groceries?

The dancing tenant was Harry. He also hated living in a tower block but he made the best of things: he sat out on his balcony and watched the world below through powerful binoculars. Harry's flat was stuffed with ornaments, no surface was free of them. Photographs of his friends and relations hung on the walls and dainty crocheted bits and pieces were arranged on the arms and backs of the three-piece suite. Harry was mortified when I told him of Mrs Bradshaw's complaint. Yes, he did dance at night. His friend came round and they danced to the Big Bands on the record player. They usually rolled the carpet back but now they knew that they were causing a disturbance they would leave the carpet where it was. Should he go down and apologise to the lady? He was a charmer, he was handsome, and he knew it. When I was fed up I used to go and see him and he would make me laugh. His daughter lived in Cornwall and his son was in Canada. He received letters from them every week without fail and he spent a month a year with his daughter. He was a happy man.

When he died I rang his daughter to give her my condolences. She knew who I was, Harry had written to say the community worker was supposed to be looking after him, but he suspected that in fact he was looking after *her*.

She asked me to arrange for some boxes and tea chests to be taken to Harry's flat. She was coming down for the funeral and would take some of Harry's things back with her in a van. I did as she'd asked.

It was eerie in his flat, like the *Marie Celeste* – an unfinished meal on the kitchen table, an unmade bed with the indentation of Harry's head on the pillow. I was washing some dirty pots when the doorbell rang – it was Harry's best friend, his dancing partner. A man in his late sixties. He and Harry had been lovers for years. He overheard the news about Harry's death in a supermarket. Their long affair had been a secret from both their families. When he heard that the daughter was expected that day he told me that Harry had a large collection of homosexual pornography hidden around his flat. In a panic we began to search for and then fling books and photographs and magazines into the boxes I had brought with me. Between us we carried the boxes down in the lift, we then staggered across waste ground to a skip provided by the council for the tenants' more innocent rubbish. Thank God it was Keep Britain Tidy week.

When the daughter came I helped her to pack away the cheap and innocent ornaments into the boxes. I hovered nervously as she opened each drawer and cupboard, had I overlooked a box of erotic photographs? Were there Scandinavian magazines lurking somewhere waiting to be found by this most respectable of daughters? She must have thought she was in the presence of a mad-woman.

She hadn't cried throughout the ordeal of sifting through her father's possessions, but when we had finished, when his clothes and his furniture had been allocated to various charities and his personal papers had been read and bundled together, that's when she began to cry. Because her father had not left a penny and he had left no provision for his funeral. There were no insurance policies: Harry was lying in the Co-op funeral parlour under false pretences. The government death grant was only thirty pounds in 1978 and the cost of a very basic funeral was £200.

Harry had been dead for two days and had already clocked up this government grant. His furniture was worn and unfashionable and would fetch very little on the second-hand market. There were no valuable family heirlooms; Harry had worked on the railways.

Because of Mrs Bradshaw, I was conversant with the funeral service provided by the council: outside normal hours a plain van took the corpse to the crematorium, a clergyman said a few words, the body was burnt and the ashes were scattered. There

68

was no guarantee that the ashes would not be mixed with those of the other, impecunious, corpses. I hesitantly mentioned the council option. Harry's daughter instantly dismissed it. Her father had been popular, she had already invited family and friends, they were coming from all over Britain, and her brother was coming from Canada. How could these grieving people follow a grey van on Harry's last journey?

Couldn't the brother help?

No, she said, he'd borrowed the money for his air ticket, he was already heavily in debt. And she had no savings but she *must* give her father a proper funeral with a hearse and cars for the mourners, an announcement in the *Leicester Mercury* and a good after-funeral meal. She would have to take out a bank loan. Pretend the money was needed for house improvements.

I didn't go to the funeral, my eldest son was ill with bronchitis, I don't know if Harry's lover attended and there was nobody I could ask. When I saw him in the local supermarket he would turn away. I embarrassed him.

Mrs Bradshaw became angry with me; my visits became less frequent. In her eyes I was a complete failure. She was offended because nobody wanted her body. One day against my advice she cashed in her insurance policy. She got less than sixty pounds. She bought herself a winter coat (though she never

69

went out) and put a deposit down on a new bed. I arranged for her old bed and its stinking mattress to be collected by the council special squad, whose unfortunate task it is to clean up after the more squalid tenants. I arranged for the new bed to be delivered and it was the last thing I ever did for Mrs Bradshaw. I left community work.

But I can't forget her showing me the garments she had put aside for her funeral – the lovely linen nightie trimmed at the wrists and collar with lace and the folded silk stockings lying waiting in their cellophane wrapper. I don't know if she wore them. I don't know if Tony forked out for a decent funeral. I don't know if she was cremated on the council because to my eternal shame, and, in spite of promising to do so, I never visited her again.

Mr Smith's privatised penis

SINCE THEY had privatised the pavements it was very difficult for Mr Smith to get to work. He had no car and it was forbidden to walk in the road, so he was forced to trespass in people's gardens and climb over their walls. There had already been complaints from his better-off neighbours; but what was he to do? He couldn't afford to pay Private Pavements Ltd for the privilege of walking on their footpaths, and anyway he resented doing so. Mr Smith remembered a time when he could stroll along any pavement he liked for as long as he chose without it costing him a penny. And what's more, he could inhale as much fresh air as he pleased, he used to breathe in great fat gobfuls of the stuff. In those days he was not required to wear an enclosed breathing hood with its meter and its red lettering, which shouted 'Private Air PLC.'

The hoods were very cumbersome to wear around the house and Mr Smith often removed his; he slept much better without it. However he dare not do this too often. Private Air PLC were entitled to cut off his supplies; there had been many disconnections lately. The crematoriums were working twenty-four hours a day.

Mr Smith looked through a thin gap in his curtains at the sunshine in his front garden. He would have liked to throw back his curtains and let the warm bright light flood into his gloomy room, but he resisted the temptation. The sunshine meter on the wall was extraordinarily sensitive to light and last quarter's bill had still not been paid; Mrs Smith had gone mad one glorious day in June and had opened the patio doors. 'Bugger it,' she had shouted when he had remonstrated with her, 'I can't live without sunshine and fresh air.' Later, when the bill from Sun and Light Ltd had come, she had apologised for her mad profligacy with these natural elements.

When a consortium of multi-national companies had bought the sun – that big burning thing in the sky – Mr Smith had thought it was a bit much and had written to the local newspaper to complain. He concluded his letter with a rhetorical question: 'What will be next, I wonder, will it be the very air we breathe?'

A year later it *was* the very air Mr Smith breathed. It wasn't fair. He didn't earn much since Work Enterprise had bought all the work in the country and had cut his wages. In fact, he was getting a bit worried about money since his savings had gone on one horrific bill to Water Ltd, the result of a broken water main outside his house. He shared this cracked pipe with the old lady next door but she had cravenly committed suicide ten minutes after opening *her* bill, leaving Mr Smith to pay for the lot. He was seriously considering having the pipe removed. There was a privatised river not far away, perhaps he could sneak a few buckets of river water at dead of night. Mrs Smith and he hardly washed themselves or their clothes anymore and river water would be safe to drink if it was boiled, wouldn't it?

Mr Smith looked at his watch and hurried upstairs to wake his wife, she was also extravagant with sleep. If he left her alone she would slumber on for as long as seven hours a night. He shook her arm and she woke. The meter on her arm (property of Sleep and Doze Co Ltd) clicked off, she sat up in bed and removed her Private Air PLC breathing hood to kiss her husband. Mr Smith kissed her neck and her breasts and her belly. He couldn't stop himself and the meter on his penis was soon ticking away merrily. 'Oh, sod the expense,' he thought, as he began to make love to his dirty but beloved wife.

About the Author

SUE TOWNSEND has written many plays, including *Bazaar and Rummage* and *The Great Celestial Cow*. She has also written several works of fiction, including *The Secret Diary of Adrian Mole Aged 13³/4*, *The Growing Pains of Adrian Mole* and *Rebuilding Coventry*. *The Secret Diary of Adrian Mole Aged 13³/4* has been adapted for the stage, radio and television, and Sue Townsend's television work includes a series for Channel Four entitled *The Refuge*.

CHATTO
Counter*Blasts*

Also available in bookshops now:-

Counter*Blasts* to be published in 1990 include:-

Christopher Hitchens on the Monarchy
Tessa Blackstone on prisons and penal reform
Douglas Dunn on Poll Tax
Ludovic Kennedy on euthanasia
Adam Mars-Jones on Venus Envy
Adam Lively on sovereignty
Margaret Drabble on property and mortgage tax relief
Ronald Dworkin on a Bill of Rights for Britain

Plus pamphlets from Michael Holroyd, Harold Evans, Hanif
Kureishi, Michael Ignatieff, Edward Mortimer and Susannah Clapp

If you want to join in the debate, and if you want to know more
about **Counter*Blasts***, the writers and the issues, then write to:

Random House UK Ltd, Freepost 5066, Dept MH, London
WC1B 3BR